Your
Wonderful World
of SCIENCE

By MAE and IRA FREEMAN

Illustrated by René Martin

SCHOLASTIC BOOK SERVICES

NEW YORK · TORONTO · LONDON · AUCKLAND · SYDNEY

You may also want to read

THE SUN, THE MOON, AND THE STARS

by Mae and Ira Freeman

Copyright © 1957 by Mae and Ira Freeman. This edition is published by Scholastic Book
Services, a division of Scholastic Magazines, Inc., by arrangement with Random House, Inc.

9th printing .... February 1970

Printed in the U.S.A.

CONTENTS

Look at Our World

PRETEND you have a space ship of your own. It stands in your back yard, ready to take you on a trip far out into space. But before you climb in, look all around you.

The world around you seems like a big, flat plate. The plate has many things on it. It has

The world around you seems like a big flat plate.

your house and your garden, your school and your town. And you know that it holds far-away cities, and mountains and oceans, too.

Is the earth as flat as it looks? Is it really as flat as a plate? You cannot tell, just by sitting in your back yard.

You could see more of the world from the roof of a tall building. And you could see for miles and miles from the top of a high mountain. But you would see only a small part of the world.

There is only one thing to do. Let your space ship take you far up into the sky. Then you will be able to look back and see all of the earth at once.

Let your space ship take you far out into the sky.

So, push the starter. The jets flash and roar. Off you go into space, as fast as lightning. In a wink, you are thousands of miles out in space.

Now look down at the earth. How different your world looks when you see it from so far away! It is not like a plate. It is not flat at all. It is really ROUND. It looks like a smooth, shiny ball.

Watch the ball for a little while. You will see something interesting. The earth is slowly, slowly turning all the time.

Now your space ship zooms off for the trip back home. The earth begins to look bigger and bigger because you are getting nearer to it. It looks blue and smooth and shiny. There are

From your space ship, the earth looks like a ball.

some greenish-brown patches here and there. As you get closer, you can see that the patches are not all smooth. Some of them are fuzzy and wrinkled.

All over the round earth you can see small white fluffs, like little bits of cotton.

This bright ball does not look like the earth you know so well. It is hard to believe that there are houses and trees and people on it.

All the time your space ship is bringing you nearer to the earth. You begin to see many things that you know.

Now you can see why most of the ball looked blue. The blue is the water of the oceans. They cover most of the earth. The greenish-brown

Clouds around the earth look like fluffy cotton.

As you come closer, you can see wrinkles in the earth.

patches are land. And what about the little wrinkles in the patches? As you come closer, you see that they are really tall mountains.

You find out that the white fluffs are clouds in the sky. Your space ship must dive through them to bring you safely to your back yard.

How good it is to be back home again, where everything looks right! Of course, you know much more about your world now that you have seen it from far away.

Now you know that the earth is round, like a ball. Now you know that water covers most of it. And you know that your world is so huge that the tallest mountains are only little wrinkles in its skin.

Soon you can see the wrinkles are tall mountains.

When the Earth Was New

Our earth is very, very old—much older than we can imagine.

When the earth was first formed, it was very hot. It was so hot that everything was all melted. Even such things as iron and rock were soft and runny. They flowed like syrup.

The earth was just a soft, sizzling ball. It was hotter than a furnace.

Slowly the earth cooled. It took a very long time. As the earth became cooler, a hard crust

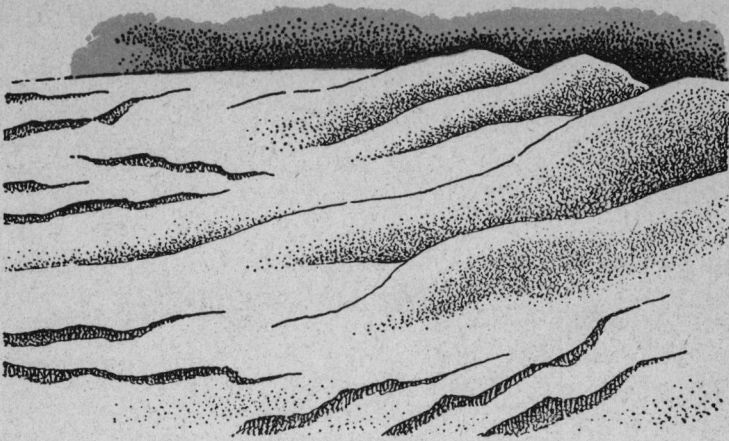

The rock crust folded upward like crumpled paper.

formed all around it. The crust was made of cooled-off rock. The earth was no longer as hot as fire, but it was still much too hot for anything to live on it.

A long time went by. In some places, great cracks could be seen as the rock crust moved. In other places, the crust folded upward like a piece of crumpled paper. The folded parts made the mountains.

Air and steam squirted out through the cracks from deep inside the earth. Thick clouds of steam filled the sky. No sunlight could come through.

The earth kept cooling off. The cooling made the steam gather together into tiny drops of water. The drops became bigger and heavier, until they fell to earth as rain. What a rainstorm it was! For years and years, great floods of water poured down.

Air and steam rose from cracks inside the earth.

As the drops became bigger, they fell as rain.

The water ran into all the low places. That is how the oceans and lakes were formed.

When the steam was gone, the air was clear. Sunshine came through to the earth at last.

Our earth still has its crust of solid rock all around it. In many places it is covered by soil, where grass and trees and farm crops grow.

The rock crust is under everything. It is under the clay at the bottom of a river. It is under the sand at the beach, and it is under the ocean, too.

How did the rock crust get covered up? Some of the rock itself was changed into sand and clay and soil. It took a long, long time for this to happen.

Water ran into low places and formed oceans and lakes.

The Rocks Wear Down

WHEN things are heated, they spread out and get just a little bigger. When things are cooled, they shrink and get a little smaller.

This happens to rocks, too. Heat makes them get bigger, and cold makes them shrink. The changes are so very tiny that you cannot see the difference. But sometimes they make a huge rock crack and split into smaller pieces.

Freezing water pushes out and breaks the rocks.

Water runs into cracks in the rocks. The water pushes out as it freezes and helps break the rock apart. The smaller pieces of rock are called stones.

Wind and rain push stones about. They knock against each other and get worn down until they become little pebbles.

The pebbles you find at the bottom of a brook are very smooth. The running water has tumbled them along, rubbing them against each other and wearing away all their sharp edges.

In running water, pebbles are rubbed smooth.

Rocks break down into stones. Stones wear away and become pebbles. At last the pebbles are so small that they are little grains of SAND.

Weeds and grass grow in cracks in the rock and break it up still more. In winter, the weeds die and rot away. They mix with the crushed rock, and this becomes SOIL.

Some rocks wear down until they are as fine as powder. The powder packs together and changes to clay.

Weeds and grass grow in cracks and break the rocks.

Treasures in the Ground

THE earth has many treasures in it. They are called MINERALS. The word MINERAL is the name for anything that is not a plant or an animal.

There are thousands of different kinds of minerals in the earth. Most of them must be hunted for, deep in the ground. Coal and oil are minerals. So are salt and sand and iron.

Some minerals are very beautiful. People wear them in jewelry. Diamonds, emeralds and rubies are some minerals that are used in rings and necklaces.

Coal is a mineral that comes from deep in the earth. It is found between layers of rock, like the filling in a sandwich.

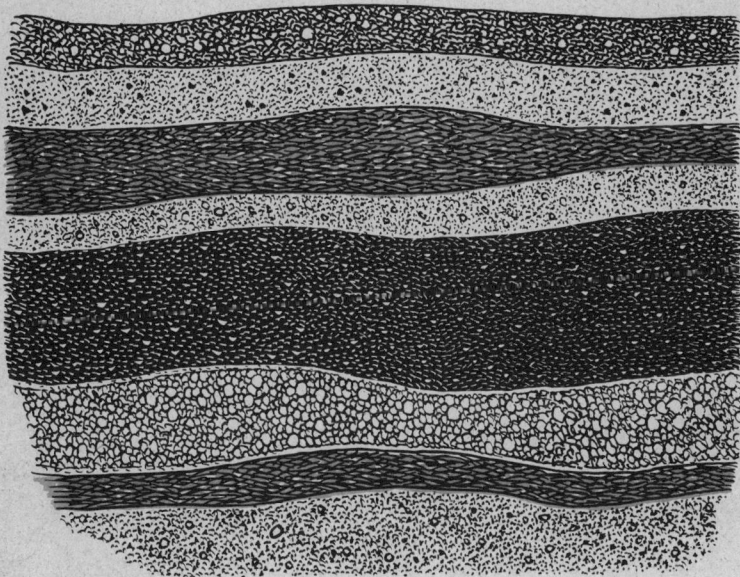

Coal is found between layers of rock.

These layers of coal came from plants and trees that grew a very long time ago. At that time the weather was hot and wet. This made everything grow into thick jungles. When the plants and trees died, they fell to the ground and were covered up by the next crop. Sometimes mud and sand and rock covered the dead plants, too.

Layers of coal came from plants that grew long ago.

The layer got thicker and thicker. It was pressed and squeezed down as it was covered more and more. Slowly, after many thousands of years, the layer of dead plants became hard, black coal.

Scientists can change coal into many other things. That is how they make aspirin tablets. Would you ever guess that these little white pills are made from coal?

We get other medicines from coal, too. And we get bright dyes for coloring our clothing and our paints. Plastic toys and nylon cloth are made of a chemical that comes from coal.

People are always finding new ways to use coal. These smudgy black lumps that come out of the earth give us many things we need.

BASALT

SANDSTONE

MARBLE

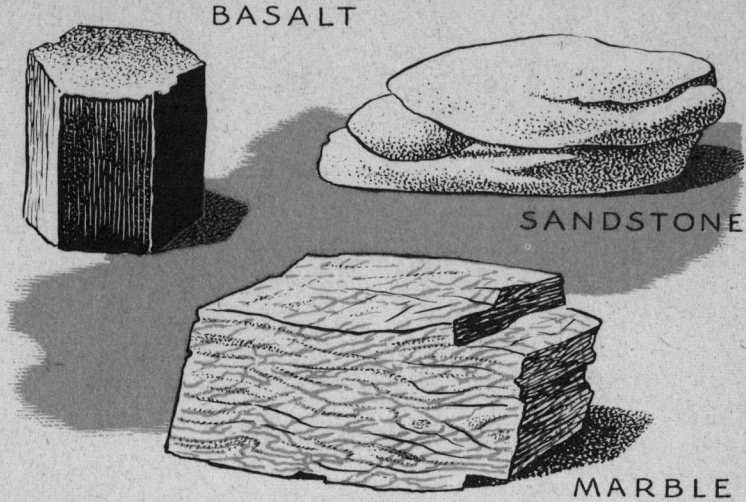

Some stones are hard and smooth; others are rough.

Have you ever collected stones? There are many kinds. You can find some that are hard and smooth. You can find some that are rough and flaky. You can find stones of almost every color. It all depends on the minerals that are in the stones.

You would never guess that many of the red stones you find have iron in them. Or that some green stones have copper in them. Some of the smooth stones you find may be marble.

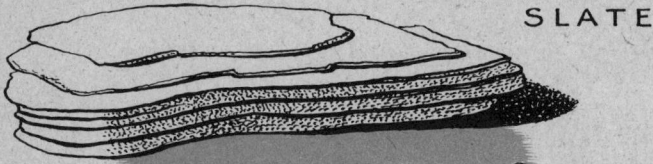

SLATE

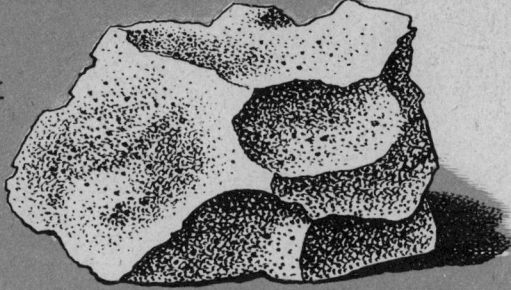

GRANITE

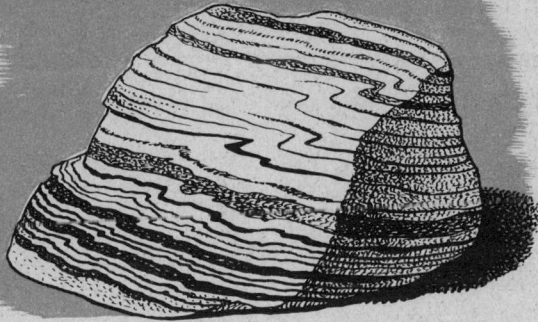

GNEISS

Some stones are known for their color and shape.

Stones can be very valuable when they have certain metals in them. You do not see any shiny metal when you look at a stone because the metal is joined with other minerals.

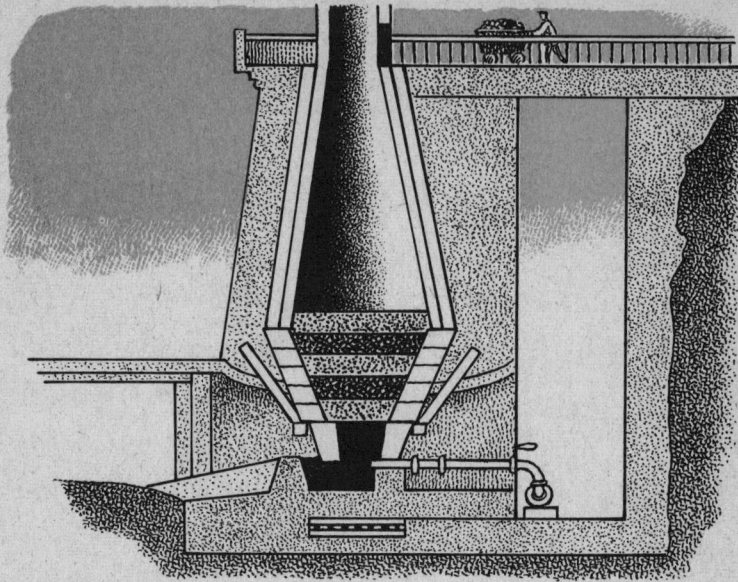

Heat in the blast furnace makes metal flow out.

There are ways to get metals out of rocks. One way is to heat the rocks in a big furnace. The heat breaks up the minerals and makes them let go of the metal. Then the melted metal is able to flow out. It is shaped into blocks as it cools and gets hard. The metal blocks are sent to factories where they can be made into many things.

That is how we get
　　steel for bridges and tall buildings . . .
　　copper for electric wires . . .
　　silver for coins and jewelry . . .
　　tin for tin cans . . .
　　and many other things.

Aluminum is a metal that we know very well. We see it and use it every day. A pound of aluminum used to cost nearly a hundred dollars. It cost so much because scientists did not know a good way to get it out of the rocks. Later, they found a way to do it easily and cheaply.

Aluminum does not rust as iron does. It is strong and light in weight. This makes it useful for building airplanes and trains.

Look around the house and see how many things are made of aluminum. Notice the pots and pans, the vacuum cleaner, the window screens. Even some candy bars are wrapped in a thin sheet of aluminum.

Food From Our Earth

THERE are minerals in the earth that we do not see at all. You cannot find them by digging. They are part of the soil itself.

Plants take up some of these minerals from the soil. The minerals become part of each plant as it grows.

A growing plant is like a chemical factory. It picks out the minerals it needs from the soil. Sunshine and water and air do their share. They

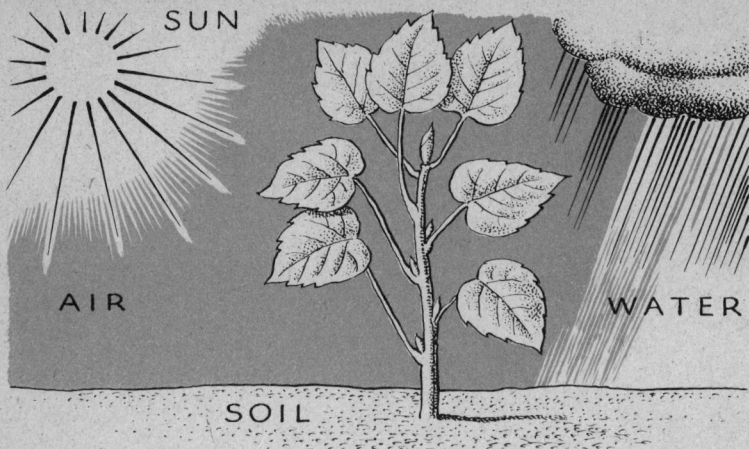

A plant uses sun, air, soil, and water to make food.

all join to build up new parts of the plant. That is how the plant grows.

We eat many plants, such as fruits and vegetables. That is how we get the minerals our bodies need to be healthy. Plants give us calcium and phosphorus to grow strong bones and teeth. They give us iron to make red blood cells.

Sometimes we eat only the roots of plants. Potatoes, carrots and beets are roots.

Sometimes we eat only the leaves of plants. Lettuce, spinach and cabbage are plant leaves.

Sometimes we eat only the seeds of plants. Peas and beans and nuts are seeds of plants.

Water All Around Us

Can you guess the name of the most precious material on earth? It is not gold, or diamonds, or oil. It is not rare at all, and you do not have to buy it. It has no color. Nothing could live without it. You drink it. Have you guessed what it is? It is WATER.

There is much more water on earth than there is land. Most of the water is in the oceans.

Try to imagine how big the oceans are. They are thousands of miles wide. They are very, very deep in some places. If you could put the highest mountain into the deepest part of the ocean, the mountain would be covered with water.

The oceans are deeper than our highest mountains.

More than half of his body is made up of water.

Look around you right now. Perhaps you do not see any water at all. But it is there, just the same.

More than half of your own body is made of water. Growing plants have water in them, too. Even things that look as hard and dry as wood have a little water in them.

Many other things look quite solid, too, but they are really full of holes. The holes are too tiny to see, and that is where the water hides. It is like the water inside a wet sponge. You cannot see the water until you squeeze it out.

There is a glass of water in each loaf of bread.

You would be surprised to know how much water there is in your food. There are three glasses of water in every quart of ice cream. Half of a hamburger is water.

A watermelon would be only as big as a baseball if you took away all the water. A loaf of bread looks quite dry, but it has a whole glass of water in it.

So you always get some water in the food that you eat. It seems like a lot, but it is not enough for good health. You must also drink several glasses of water every day.

When is water as hard as stone? When it freezes and becomes ICE.

Ice is very strong. It holds you up when you skate across a frozen pond. Eskimos in the far North build their houses out of blocks of ice.

Water becomes bigger when it turns into ice. It spreads out and takes up more room. If you put a bottle full of water outdoors on a very cold day, the water will freeze. You will see the ice sticking up out of the bottle. You may cover the bottle as tightly as you can, but you will not stop the push of the ice. It will crack the glass.

The bottle was broken by the pushing ice.

Nothing can keep water from pushing out as it freezes. Even a strong iron water pipe will be broken if water freezes in the pipe.

Sometimes there is water in cracks in the street. If the water freezes, the ice will break up the pavement.

Ice can break up huge rocks, too. Sometimes there is rain water in the holes and cracks of a rock. If the weather gets very cold, the water freezes. It must get bigger and push out. The pushing makes the rock crack and break into pieces.

Have you ever seen heaps of stones lying at the bottom of a cliff? They were once part of the big rocks above. The pieces fell when ice broke them off.

Ice breaks off stones which fall to the ground.

The Air We Breathe

THERE is something all around you that you cannot see. You cannot hold it in your hands. But when the wind blows, you know something is there because it pushes against you. It is AIR.

Would you like to feel some air? Get a small paper bag. Blow into it to make it swell up. As you finish blowing, twist the end of the bag tightly to keep the air inside.

Hold the twisted end with one hand. Press the bag with your other hand. The bag feels like a pillow. There is certainly something inside.

Is it filled with feathers? Or foam rubber? No, only AIR. Now you know that air is real, because you have felt it with your hands.

Things filled with air can be very useful. You are really riding on air when you travel in a car. Air is pumped into the tires to make them springy. Then the tires can take up the bumps in the road, and your ride is smooth and comfortable.

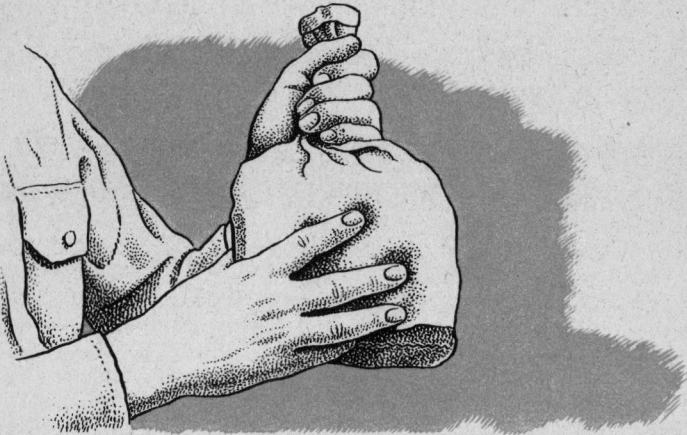

You can feel the air that fills a paper bag.

Fill the ball with air, and it will float in water.

Footballs and basketballs are filled with air to make them bounce. Without air, they have no bounce at all.

A beach ball is flat and soft before you fill it with air. It will sink if you put it into water. After you blow air into a beach ball, it becomes round and hard. Then it will float. It can hold you up easily in the water.

When air moves, it pushes against anything that is in its way. The wind rattles the windows, and it makes the trees bend and sway.

Air pushes on the sails and moves the boat ahead.

A strong breeze can push on the sails of a boat and move it swiftly across the lake.

When you fly a kite, the moving air holds it up. If the breeze stops, the kite will come down.

A bird flies by beating its wings against the air. An airplane has propellers that push against the air. It has wings that are set so the air can hold it up, just as the air holds up a kite.

There Is Water in the Air

Moving air carries many things along with it. It carries fallen leaves and scraps of paper. It carries dust and the seeds of plants. You can see these things floating along on the wind.

The air carries something else, too. It carries water. But the water is in such tiny bits that you cannot see it. Then we do not call it water. We call it WATER VAPOR.

Air always has some water vapor in it. The hot air of summer carries it. The cold air of winter carries it. There is water vapor in the air on top of a mountain, and in the air in the lowlands, too.

All the air inside every building carries water vapor. The air in your own house has almost a pailful of water in it!

When water dries away and becomes water vapor, we cannot see it any more. We say that it EVAPORATES.

As a puddle dries up, the water goes into the air.

Water is evaporating all the time. It evaporates from rivers and lakes and oceans. It evaporates from wet sidewalks and from wet floors. Indoors and outdoors, water is always changing to water vapor.

You wash your face in the morning and hang up the wet cloth. After a while, you find that the washcloth is dry. The water has gone into the air. It has evaporated.

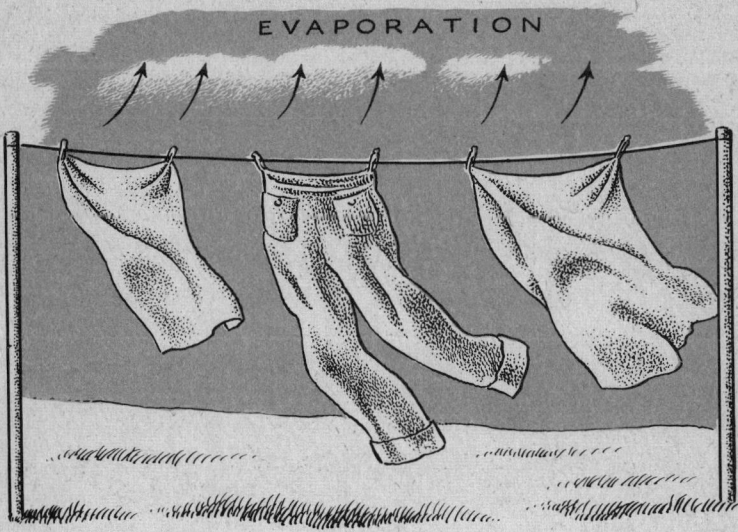

EVAPORATION

Water from the wet clothes goes into the air.

Water evaporates from anything that is wet. You come out of the water after a swim and play on the beach in the sunshine. Soon, like magic, your swimming suit is quite dry. The water has evaporated into the air.

Your bathing suit will dry very quickly when the sun is hot and bright because heat makes water evaporate faster. If the sun is not shining, the bathing suit will take much longer to dry.

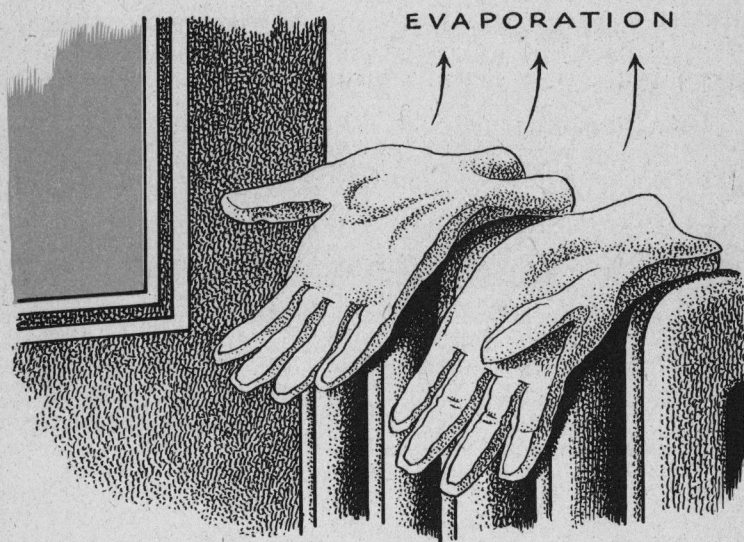

Heat makes water evaporate much faster.

Wet gloves will dry quickly if you put them on a hot radiator. Washed clothes dry much sooner in the hot sun than in a cool cellar. Outdoors the breeze helps, too. It makes the water evaporate faster.

You can watch water evaporate when a damp cloth is ironed. The iron makes a dry path as it moves across the cloth. The heat of the iron makes the water disappear into the air.

When water evaporates all by itself, it makes things feel cool. Before you get into your bath, you feel comfortable in the warm room. The warm water feels comfortable, too. But you may begin to shiver as soon as you step out of the tub. The water evaporating from your skin makes you feel cold.

The Air Makes Our Weather

WHEN you woke up this morning, you probably went to the window to look at the weather for today. Perhaps you wondered if it was a good day for baseball — or swimming — or skating.

When you ask about the weather, you are really trying to find out how the air is behaving. You cannot see the air itself, but it is easy to tell what it is doing.

What did the air tell you about itself when you looked out of the window this morning? Was it blowing fiercely, tossing snowflakes against your window? Was it filled with gray mist and falling rain? Or was it quiet and clear, letting the warm sunshine come down?

Your room stays snug and comfortable, even on a cold winter day. How can one small stove or radiator warm the whole room?

This is what happens. First, the radiator warms the air right next to it. Warmed air swells up like a balloon. It gets lighter and floats upward. As the light, warm air gets out of the way, cool air moves in to take its place.

All the air in your room keeps moving round and round in tall circles. It gets warmed and goes up. It cools off and comes down again. That is how all the air in your room is kept warm by the radiator.

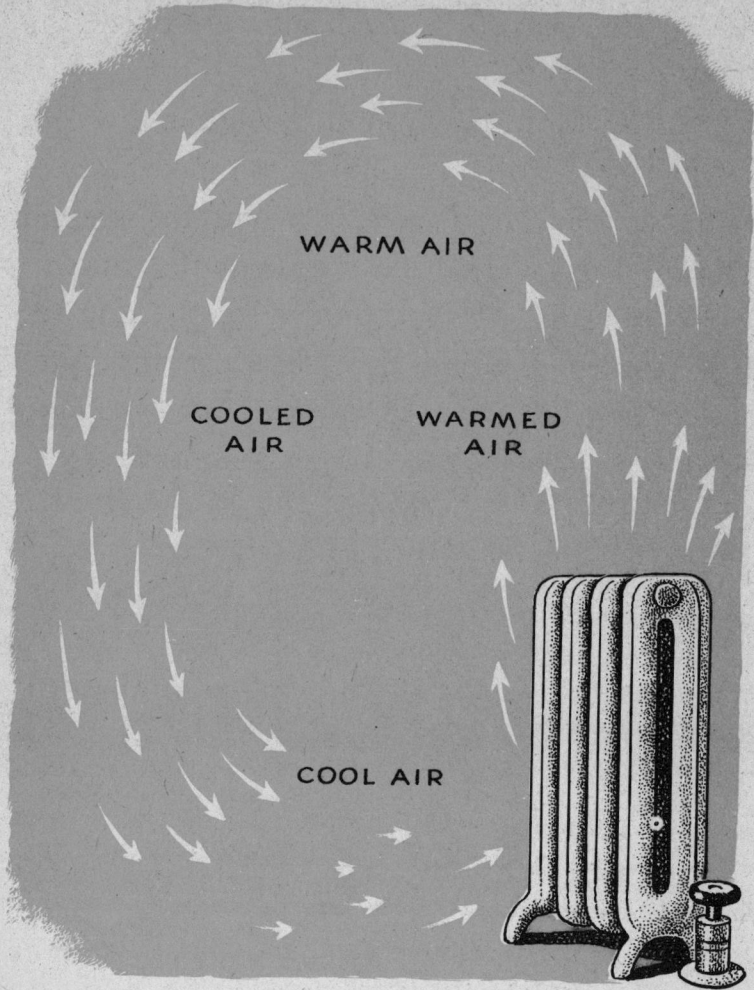

WARM AIR

COOLED
AIR

WARMED
AIR

COOL AIR

Air goes up when warmed by a hot radiator.

Indoors or outdoors, heat makes the air move. Indoors, the radiator is our heater. Outdoors, the sun is our heater.

The sun warms the ground. The ground warms the air right next to it, and the warmed air goes up. Then cool air moves in along the ground from all around. This moving air is the WIND.

Usually the cool air comes in gently, and we have pleasant breezes. But when the air rushes in, we have very strong winds, and sometimes even large, whirling storms called HURRICANES.

COOL AIR

WARMED AIR

WARMED GROUND

Air goes up when warmed by the earth.

Clouds, Rain, and Snow

WHEN air rises high into the sky, it cools off. Then it begins to lose some of its load of water vapor. The coolness makes the water vapor come out of the air and turn into many, many tiny droplets.

The droplets of water are too small to fall back to the ground. They float high above the earth. They gather together like a swarm of bees.

Sunshine makes these clouds look white.

The huge swarm of water droplets is called a
CLOUD.

Some clouds are fluffy, like puffs of white
cotton floating in the blue sky. These clouds look
white because the sun shines through them and
makes them bright.

There are days when the whole sky is covered
with thick layers of clouds. The sunlight cannot
get through them. Then the cloudy sky looks
dark and gray.

Some clouds form much higher in the sky than
the others. It is very, very cold up there. It is so
cold that the water vapor freezes. Then there are
tiny bits of ice floating in the air, instead of drops
of water. They make clouds that look like thin
trails of smoke.

Some clouds form much higher in the sky than others.

Sometimes the air high up in the sky stays cold a long time. The cold makes more and more water vapor change to water droplets. There are so many tiny droplets that they stick together and form larger drops.

The drops get bigger and heavier all the time. At last they are too heavy to float in the air. The big ones fall to earth. That is RAIN.

Each falling raindrop could tell a different story. One may have come all across the country in a cloud. It may have tossed and tumbled for many days high in the air. Another may have been in the sky for only a few minutes. Now these raindrops from far and near are coming down together.

A cloud can form right on the ground. Then we have a FOG. It is just like the clouds in the sky. But a fog is a cloud you can walk through.

Outdoors on a cold winter day, you make your own little cloud each time you breathe. The cloud from your breath fades away very quickly.

You can make a fog on a cold windowpane by breathing on it.

You can make water drops come out of the

air almost like magic. Put some ice cubes in a glass of water. Watch what happens.

Soon you see little drops of water on the outside of the glass. Where did they come from? They could not come through the hard glass from inside. The drops came from the air that was cooled by the glass.

When the drops get very big, they run down the side of the glass. It reminds you of the

On a cold day, your breath makes a little cloud.

Water on the outside of the glass comes from the air.

droplets in the clouds that become big, and fall as rain.

In winter, the air high above the earth may cool off so quickly that there is no time for rain-drops to form. SNOWFLAKES are formed instead. They are light, and float gently down through the air, like little feathers. The snowflakes pile up on the ground, and the wind sweeps them into huge snowdrifts.

Each snowflake is a tiny speck of ice. The next time it snows, let some snowflakes fall on your woolen glove. They will not melt too quickly there. Notice what pretty shapes they have.

You can see them better if you have a magnifying glass. Each snowflake has six sides or six points, but the design of each one is different. No two are ever exactly alike.

Use a magnifying glass and you will see that each snowflake has six sides or six points.

Water and Its Travels

THE water in the air always comes back to earth. It may fall as rain, or it may fall as snow that melts later.

The water from the rain or snow runs over the ground. Part of it soaks in. It soaks down into the soil and between the deep layers of rock.

In some places, the water bubbles up again through cracks in the earth. It comes out sparkling and cold, and forms a SPRING. The spring flows all the time.

A farmer is very lucky if he has a spring on his land. He can use the pure, clear water to help grow his crops. There is plenty of it for washing and drinking. If the farmer has no spring, he must dig a well and pump the water up from deep in the ground.

On the hillside, water gushes from a spring.

Water from the rain forms little brooks and streams.

Water from the rain runs over the land and down the hills. It forms little brooks that flow along and join other brooks.

The stream of water becomes deep and broad. Soon it is big enough to be called a river. Some rivers are more than a mile wide and hundreds of miles long. At last, the water of the rivers reaches the ocean.

All along, some of the water evaporates into the air. It goes up high in the sky to form clouds. Then rain falls, and down comes the water once again.

That is how the water goes back and forth, from earth to sky and from sky to earth. The story goes on, over and over, never stopping.

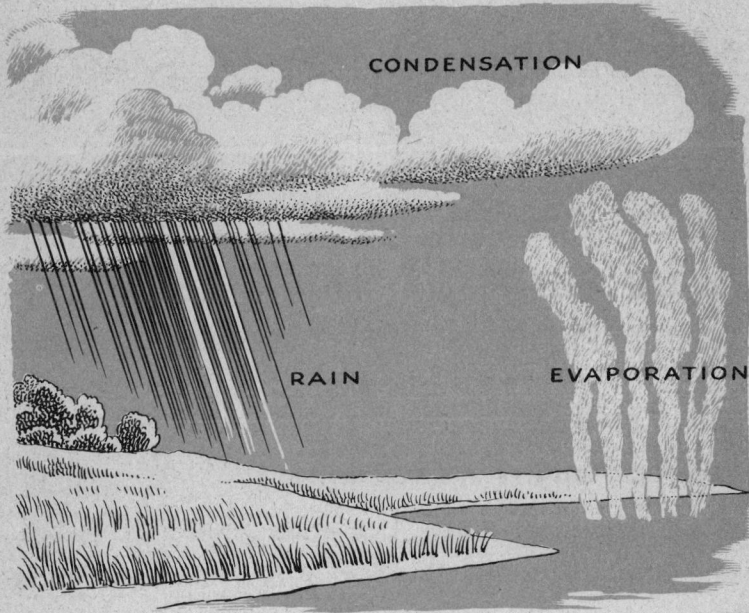

Water goes from earth to sky and back to the earth.

Fire—Friend and Enemy

You have a wonderful helper that works for you all the time. It cooks your food. It keeps your house warm. It is your good friend and can do many things for you.

But if you are careless, it can be your enemy. It can burn down your house. It can destroy forests and kill people and animals.

Its name is FIRE.

The first people on earth did not know how to make fire. They had to wait until a fire started by itself. Sometimes lightning would strike a tree in the forest. That started a fire.

The cave men would drag burning branches to the caves where they lived. They kept the fire going a long time by putting more twigs and branches on it. Sometimes they could keep the fire burning for years.

The lucky ones who had a fire were sure to be warm all winter. The fire protected them, too. It frightened away wild animals. People could sleep without fear when a fire was burning at the opening of their cave.

Cave men used fire to frighten away wild animals.

It was hard for the cave men to keep a fire going. It had to be watched all the time. They could not take the fire with them when they moved to a new hunting ground.

Then, one day, a spark flew out when someone was chipping very hard stones. The spark landed on some dry leaves, and they began to burn.

At last cave men knew how to start a fire. Now they knew that they could make sparks by knocking two stones together.

Later, people learned to make fire by rubbing sticks together. For a very long time, that was the only way they knew to start a fire.

Rubbing makes things hot. You can find this out yourself. Rub the palms of your hands together fast and hard. See how warm they get. Of course, to make a fire, you must use sharp sticks and rub them together a long time.

Today we have a much easier way to start a fire. We use matches. We still have to rub something. But just one rub is enough to set fire to the chemical material on the tip of a match stick.

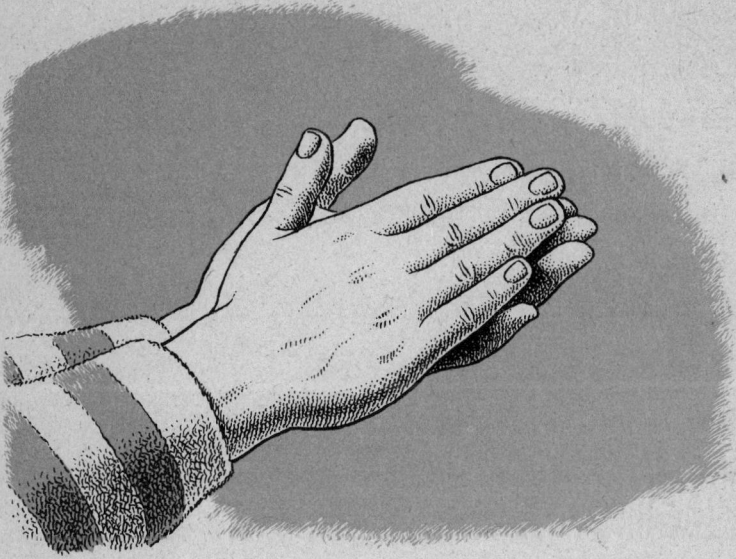

Your hands get hot as you rub them together.

At first, matches were very dangerous. They could be set on fire too easily. Sometimes they even caught fire in the box, just by rubbing on each other. Now most matches are safety matches. They burn only when struck on the outside of their own box.

As a boy, Lincoln had only an open fire for light.

Fire gives us light. It used to be the only way to light a room after the sun went down. Abraham Lincoln would read at night by the open fire. That was the only place where there was any light.

A hundred years ago people used candles for light at night. But in those times candles cost too much to be used all the time. Rich people would light their great houses by burning hundreds of candles. Sometimes the open flames started fires.

Now it is different. You snap a switch and fill your room with safe, bright electric light.

Some things burn easily. Paper and wood catch fire quickly. You can think of many other materials that will burn.

How many things can you name that will NOT burn? Remember that chimneys are made of brick, and that fireplaces are made of stone. Think of the kitchen stove, and the pots and pans on it. These will remind you of materials that do not burn.

It is lucky there are materials that cannot catch fire. They help us use fire indoors. We can put fire inside of furnaces and stoves, and keep it safely there.

Fire will not destroy the iron pot.

When the air is gone, the flame goes out.

Nothing can burn without air. Not even paper or wood. Every fire needs air to keep it going.

Suppose we light a candle and cover it with a glass jar. What do you think will happen? The candle flame will go out after just a few seconds. That is because the flame uses up the air in the jar. When this part is gone, the flame goes out.

Sometimes it is hard to keep a campfire going. But if you fan it with your cap or jacket, the fire will blaze up. Fanning brings more air into the fire.

We can put out a fire by throwing water or sand on it. The covering by water or sand shuts out the air. The fire dies quickly when it can get no more air.

The fire goes out when the sand shuts out the air.

Heat and How We Use It

WE PUT heat to work making many things. Heat can turn sand into GLASS.

Making glass is like making hard candy. In a candy factory, sugar is heated until it melts and flows like syrup. The syrup is flavored, and when it thickens it is formed into different shapes. After it hardens, each piece is a lollipop, or a peppermint stick, or some other kind of hard candy.

In this furnace, sand is melted and made into glass.

In a glass factory, sand is melted and changes to glass. It can be poured or pressed into any shape while it is still soft. The glass gets very hard as it cools.

All glass comes from melted sand. That is how we get glass for windowpanes, bottles, lamps, marbles and many other things.

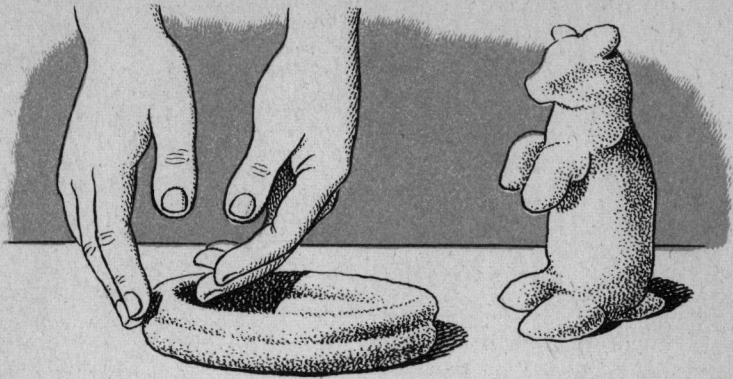

When wet, clay can be made into many different shapes.

It is fun to make things out of clay, because you can form clay into any shape you want. You can make ash trays or animals or dolls.

The clay is shaped while it is wet. Then it is left to dry. The clay gets hard, but it breaks and crumbles very easily. Things made of clay will keep longer if they are baked in a special oven. The heat makes the clay as hard as stone.

That is how bricks are made. Blocks of clay are baked in a huge oven. The bricks must stay in the oven two or three days to make them hard and strong.

Oven heat makes the clay figures as hard as stone.

Heat is something you cannot see. The water in a bowl looks the same whether it is hot or cold. You have to dip your finger in it to find out.

We can tell exactly how hot or cold things are by measuring their TEMPERATURE. Anything that is hot has a high temperature. Anything that is cold has a low temperature.

A THERMOMETER tells us the temperature, just as a clock tells us the time. A clock has numbers

Thermometers tell temperature just as clocks tell time.

for the hours of the day, and a thermometer has numbers for the DEGREES of temperature.

The thermometer outside your door tells the temperature of the air. The temperature of the air may be 100 degrees or more on a hot summer day. It may go down to 5 degrees on a cold day in winter. It may go even lower.

Some things are VERY COLD. Dry ice is 100 degrees below zero. The ice-cream man uses dry ice to keep his ice-cream bars frozen hard.

Some things are VERY HOT. The temperature of a candle flame is hundreds of degrees. And inside the sun, the temperature is millions of degrees!

The Sun

THERE is a big, glowing ball in the sky. It is much hotter and brighter than anything on earth. It is so big that more than a million earths could fit inside it. It is the SUN.

The sun is really a star. It is our own special star. All the other stars are glowing balls like our sun, but they are much farther away from the earth. They are so far away that they seem to be only tiny, twinkling lights.

EDGE OF SUN

☉ EARTH

More than a million earths could fit into the sun.

The sun looks bigger and brighter than any other star because it is so much nearer to us. Even so, it would take months for the fastest rocket to get to the sun.

Our earth is always turning. It takes a whole day to go around once. You do not feel the slow turning at all. It seems as if the earth is really quite still.

Wherever you are on earth, the turning makes you see different parts of the sky. Round and round the earth goes. When your part of the earth faces the sun, it is DAY. When your part of the earth is turned away from the sun, it is NIGHT.

Every place in the world gets its chance to face the sun. At night when it is dark and you are asleep, people on the other side of the earth are awake and busy in bright daylight. The earth keeps turning. Soon it is time for you to come into the sunlight and begin a new day.

As the earth turns, new parts come into daylight.

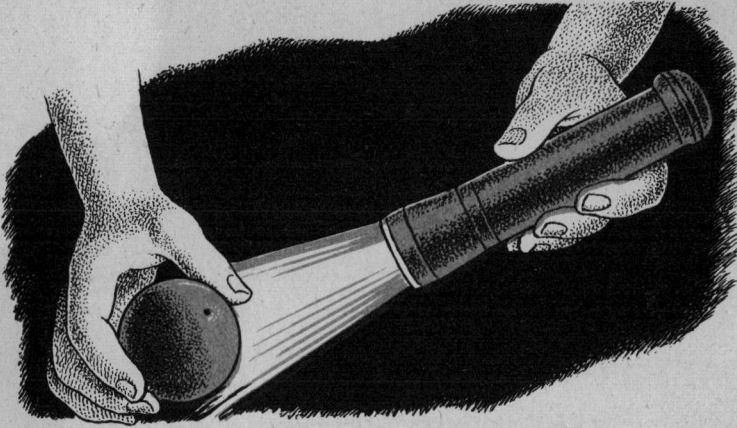

The flashlight shines on the turning ball as the sun shines on the turning earth.

You can play sun-and-earth with a ball and a flashlight. The flashlight is the sun. The ball is the earth. Mark a black dot on the ball. The dot is YOU.

Slowly turn the ball as the flashlight shines on it. See how the dot moves around, into the light and then out of the light.

That is how the turning of the earth brings day and night to our world.

INDEX